# THE GOURMET KITCHEN —
# OLIVE &
# OTHER OILS

WRITTEN BY GINA STEER
ILLUSTRATED BY HILARY DOWNING

THE
APPLE
PRESS

A QUARTO BOOK

Published by The Apple Press
6 Blundell Street
London N7 9BH

ISBN 1-85076-541-3

This book was designed and produced by
Quarto Publishing plc
The Old Brewery, 6 Blundell Street
London N7 9BH

Editors: Kate Kirby, Laura Washburn, Susan Ward
Art Editor: Mark Stevens
Designer: Julie Francis
Art Director: Moira Clinch
Editorial Director: Sophie Collins

Typeset in Great Britain by West End Studios, Eastbourne, UK
Manufactured in Hong Kong by Regent Publishing Services Ltd.
Printed in China by Leefung-Asco Printers Ltd.

# *Contents*

# INTRODUCTION

Oil has been an essential ingredient throughout history. Investigations along the Nile Valley have led archaeologists to believe that the ancient Egyptians extracted oil from the radish. Sesame oil has always been used extensively in the Middle East, while the first recorded use of sunflower oil was by the Native Americans. These days olive oil is one of the most important ingredients in Italian cuisine and throughout the Mediterranean — used in soups, pasta sauces, vegetable dishes and in most other prepared foods. Oil is also the main component in mayonnaise and in vinaigrette dressings. The type of oil used is of paramount importance, since well chosen high-quality oils can transform ordinary ingredients into 'food for the gods'.

Oil is also important in baking, for brushing over meat prior to cooking, or for marinating to tenderise or add flavour. All manner of foods — from chips to churros — are cooked in deep or shallow baths of oil and special oils are also used in some beauty products.

It's not that many years ago, that the variety of oils available was very limited. Olive oil and other flavoured oils were virtually unheard of outside their countries of origin. Now, with air travel accessible to all, and with today's emphasis on healthy eating, the wide flavourful family of cooking oils has come into its own.

## Olive Oil

Olive oil is becoming increasingly popular in Britain, as more and more people are learning to love its distinctive fruity flavour and to explore its versatility. But olive oil's new status as one of the fashionable staples of the 1990s is also partly due to its recently discovered health benefits.

People in Mediterranean countries traditionally have a low incidence of heart disease and cancer, and it now appears that this is partly due to the amount of olive

oil in their diet. Recent research has shown that the mono-unsaturated fatty acids in olive oil reduce the level of 'bad' cholesterol in the body without reducing the beneficial HDL cholesterol, and this helps prevent heart disease. It seems that the fatty acids contained in olive oil also help the body to resist cancer-causing agents. Furthermore, because olive oil is cold pressed antioxidants — which play a vital role in fighting disease — are preserved intact.

Olives are one of the oldest fruits known to civilisation. The cultivation of olive trees is believed to have begun around 6000 BC. Today there are 24 million acres planted with over 800 million olive trees. Almost all of these are in Italy, Greece, Spain, Portugal and France — countries that have the ideal climate for the production of olives.

Not only the climate but also the soil and the method of cultivation affect the oil — and there are at least 60 different varieties. Like wine, oils vary immensely, from mild sweet oils with a light fruity flavour, to strong pungent oils with a full-bodied sometimes almost peppery taste. The colour also varies considerably, from pale gold or green to deeper more intense shades. Generally, the darker the oil the stronger the flavour.

Olives are normally hand picked to prevent bruising, then they are given a single 'cold' pressing to release the oil. The harvested olives are ground to a thick paste, which is then pressed at room temperature until all the liquid is extracted. After it has been filtered, the oil is tasted and rated according to the following categories:

**Extra-Virgin Olive Oil** Produced in small quantities only, this is the most expensive of all olive oils and is much prized for its superb flavour and aroma. It can vary in colour from very pale green to deep yellow, depending on origin. It has an acidity level of not more than 1 percent.

**Virgin Olive Oil** This does not have to meet such exacting standards as extra-virgin oil. It has an acidity level of not more than 1-3.3 percent.

**Pure Olive Oil** This is a blend of refined virgin olive oil and virgin olive oil. The refined oil is made by removing the impurities from oils that weren't quite good enough to be rated as virgin or extra-virgin. This produces a blander oil so it is blended with unrefined virgin oil.

7

# Other Oils for Flavouring

Oil is extracted from many different plants, fruits, seeds and nuts. The wealth of resulting flavours and aromas is a gourmet's delight. Some are only suitable for specific purposes; an example is almond oil used in confectionery and baking. Other varieties such as sunflower oil are used extensively in hot and cold savoury dishes, salads and marinades.

Though olive oil is number one for flavour and universal popularity, other oils notable for distinctive taste and aroma are derived from nuts or seeds — hazelnut, walnut and sesame. Used mainly for salad dressings or quick stir-fry dishes, their flavour changes and disappears if heated too high or too long. Sesame oil, of paramount importance in both hot and cold Oriental dishes, is therefore usually added with a quick burst of heat at the end of cooking to give an extra nutty tang.

A whole range of special oils prized for their flavouring properties is now appearing on supermarket and delicatessen shelves. Some have been combined with rapeseed. Herbs and spices such as basil, rosemary, roasted garlic, chillies, mustard seeds and other inspirations have been added to the cook's repertoire of oils. Try browsing in the relevant section of your local shop or deli and be stimulated by oils such as 'stir-fry oil' — a combination of rapeseed, olive, sesame and garlic oils, flavoured with ginger, dried chillies, black peppercorns and mustard seeds; or Mediterranean-flavoured oil, an extravagant concoction of rapeseed, olive, garlic and basil oils, spiked with thyme, bay leaf and peppercorns.

## *Other Oils for Cooking*

Most oils have two distinctive characteristics: they tend to break down when heated to high temperatures, and to harden and separate in cold weather or if kept in a refrigerator. Manufacturers have developed the process of 'winterizing'. This artificially freezes the oil and precipitates the solids. The remaining oil is then sold as salad — not cooking — oil.

Oils used mainly for cooking must remain stable when heated. Though they can contain stabilisers (to counteract the separation of solids) and emulsifiers (to help prevent food from sticking to pans and water droplets from spitting), these

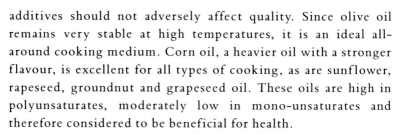

additives should not adversely affect quality. Since olive oil remains very stable at high temperatures, it is an ideal all-around cooking medium. Corn oil, a heavier oil with a stronger flavour, is excellent for all types of cooking, as are sunflower, rapeseed, groundnut and grapeseed oil. These oils are high in polyunsaturates, moderately low in mono-unsaturates and therefore considered to be beneficial for health.

Sunflower oil is tailor-made both for cooking and for salad dressings since its mild taste will not mask others.

Safflower and rapeseed oils are higher in polyunsaturates than any other oil. For this reason they are often specified for special diets and in 'health' salads. If untreated they can develop a fishy taste when heated, so stabilisers are usually added. Their unobtrusive flavours enable them to combine well with other oils or ingredients.

# Storing & Flavouring Oils

Olive oil loses its colour and aroma if exposed to the light. Although bottles do not need to be kept in the refrigerator, they should be tightly capped and stored in a cool dark place. This should ensure that the oil survives up to two years. If the temperature drops and the oil solidifies, simply remove the oil to a warmer place to liquefy before use.

Nut oils should be bought sparingly, kept in a cool dark place or a refrigerator and used quickly. Once opened they tend to go rancid within weeks. Unopened and stored correctly they will keep for up to 6 months. Avoid buying bottles with a cork stopper as the oil — particularly walnut and hazelnut oils — will oxidise if not used quickly. Less pungent oils such as sunflower, safflower and rapeseed will last indefinitely unopened. Once opened, use within a reasonable length of time.

If you wish to experiment in making your own flavoured oil, try steeping fresh herbs such as basil, rosemary, tarragon or lemon grass in olive oil. Sterilise an attractive jar, drop in your chosen herb and carefully fill with olive oil. Seal well and leave in the refrigerator for about 3–4 weeks. Once opened, use as quickly as possible. Spices such as star anise, peppercorns, chillies, coriander seeds and cumin seeds can also be used. Home-made flavoured oils should be kept in the refrigerator.

# STARTERS

## Tomato & Rosemary Focaccia

310g/11oz strong plain flour
½ teaspoon salt
7g/¼oz easy-blend yeast
3 tablespoons olive oil
210ml/7floz warm water

### Topping

1 x 285g/10½oz jar oil-packed sun-dried tomatoes,
drained and roughly chopped
4 tablespoons finely chopped fresh rosemary
30g/1oz Parmesan cheese, grated
4–5 tablespoons olive oil
About ½ teaspoon sea salt

Combine the flour and salt in a mixing bowl. Stir in the yeast and then the olive oil. Gradually stir in sufficient warm water to form a soft dough. Turn out on to a lightly floured surface and knead gently until smooth and pliable. Place the dough in a clean lightly oiled bowl, cover with a tea towel or oiled cling film, and leave in a warm place for 40 minutes or until the dough has doubled in size.

Preheat the oven to 190°C/375°F/gas mark 5. Turn the dough out on to a lightly floured surface, knock it back using your knuckles and knead again for 5 minutes. Divide the dough in half. Shape each half into a flat round about 20cm/8in in diameter. Place on two lightly oiled baking sheets.

Push the pieces of sun-dried tomatoes into the surface of the dough, making definite indentations as you do so. Sprinkle the tops with rosemary and Parmesan cheese. Drizzle with olive oil and sprinkle with sea salt to taste. Bake for 15-20 minutes or until the loaves are a pale golden brown color. Serve warm. *Makes 2 loaves.*

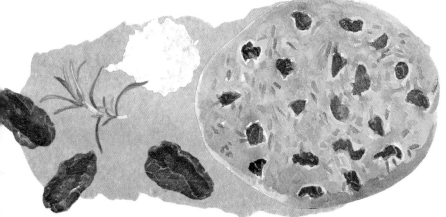

# Sautéed Asparagus with Parma Ham

*450g/1lb fresh asparagus, trimmed*
*4 tablespoons virgin olive oil*
*1 tablespoon sherry vinegar or balsamic vinegar*
*115g/4oz Parma ham, trimmed and sliced into 1cm/½in strips*
*8–12 large shavings of pecorino cheese*
*Pinch of sea salt and ¼ teaspoon freshly ground black pepper*
*2 cherry tomatoes, halved*
*Few basil sprigs*

*C*ut the asparagus diagonally into 5cm/2in lengths. Heat the oil in a frying pan over moderate heat, then gently sauté the asparagus for 3–4 minutes or until just tender. Add vinegar and Parma ham and heat through for a further 1 minute. Remove from heat, and arrange on a serving platter. Scatter the cheese shavings over the asparagus and sprinkle with the salt and pepper. Garnish with the cherry tomatoes and basil sprigs. *Serves 4.*

# Pecan Cherry Tomatoes

*340g/12oz large firm cherry tomatoes*
*3 tablespoons walnut oil*
*85g/3oz fresh chanterelle mushrooms, wiped and finely chopped*
*4 spring onions, trimmed and finely chopped*
*30g/1oz pecan nut or walnut halves, chopped*
*1 teaspoon clear acacia honey*
*2 tablespoons chopped fresh coriander*
*Pinch of salt and ¼ teaspoon freshly ground black pepper*
*60g/2oz salad leaves*
*Fresh coriander leaves to garnish*

*W*ipe or wash the tomatoes and cut a thin slice from the top. Scoop out the centres. (Reserve the flesh to use in sauces.) Heat the oil in a frying pan over moderate heat, then sauté the mushrooms for 2 minutes. Add the spring onions and pecans and continue to sauté for a further 2 minutes. Remove from the heat and stir in the honey, coriander and the seasoning. Fill the tomato shells with the mixture and serve on a bed of salad leaves, garnished with fresh coriander leaves. *Serves 4.*

# Salmon Bites

*180g/6oz halloumi, feta or other hard salty cheese, cubed*
*340g/12oz fresh salmon fillet, skinned and cubed*
*6 tablespoons extra-virgin olive oil or Porcini oil*
*4 tablespoons lime juice*
*1 tablespoon chopped fresh dill*
*Pinch of salt and ¼ teaspoon freshly ground black pepper*
*1 lime, cut into small wedges*
*4 lime twists*
*Few dill sprigs*

*P*lace the cheese and salmon in a shallow dish. Mix together the oil, lime juice, chopped dill and seasoning. Pour this marinade over the cheese and fish. Cover and chill for 1 hour.

Preheat the grill to high. Drain the cheese and salmon and thread on small skewers with the lime wedges. Grill for 3–4 minutes, turning at least once and brushing with the remaining marinade. Garnish with the lime twists and dill sprigs and serve. *Serves 4.*

# *Thai Scallops*

*8–12 scallops per person, with shells*

*1–2 fresh green chillies, chopped*

*2 cloves garlic, crushed*

*2 stalks lemon grass, trimmed and chopped*

*3 tablespoons finely chopped fresh coriander*

*4 tablespoons stir-fry oil*

*1 tablespoon soy sauce*

*3 tablespoons rice vinegar*

*½ teaspoon grated lime zest*

*3 green chillies, cut into flowers and chilled in ice water*

Clean the scallops and set aside. Scrub the scallop shells, and place in an oven heated to 95°C/200°F/gas mark ¼ to dry, for 5 minutes.

Place the scallops in a shallow dish. Mix together the chopped chillies, garlic, lemon grass, coriander, 3 tablespoons of the oil, the soy sauce and vinegar. Pour this mixture over the scallops, cover and chill for 1 hour. Stir occasionally.

Heat the remaining oil in a wok. Drain the scallops, then stir-fry over high heat for 2–3 minutes or until cooked. Arrange on the shells (or in small ramekins), garnish with the lime zest and the chilli flowers and serve. *Serves 4.*

# Parsley & Lemon Dip

*2 tablespoons chopped fresh parsley*
*1 tablespoon chopped fresh mint*
*Grated zest of ½ large lemon*
*2 cloves garlic, crushed*
*3 tablespoons virgin olive oil or lemon-flavoured oil*
*6 tablespoons plain yogurt*
*2–3 tablespoons toasted pine nuts*
*¼ teaspoon freshly ground black pepper*

*B*lend the parsley, mint, lemon zest, garlic and oil together in a food processor to form a thick paste. Gradually blend in the yogurt until you have a thick dipping consistency. Stir in the pine nuts and pepper. Chill. Serve with crudités or spread on to thick slices of toasted ciabatta or country-style bread that has been drizzled with extra oil. *Makes 150ml/¼ pint.*

# Tomato & Basil Crostini

6 tablespoons virgin olive oil

115g/4oz oyster mushrooms, wiped and chopped

3 plum tomatoes, peeled, seeded, drained and chopped

115g/4oz Parma ham, chopped

1 tablespoon chopped fresh basil

1/4 teaspoon freshly ground black pepper

1 ciabatta loaf or other thick-textured bread

Few basil sprigs

Pour 3 tablespoons of the oil into a small frying pan and sauté the mushrooms over moderate heat for 2 minutes. Add the plum tomatoes, Parma ham, the chopped basil and pepper. Stir for 2 minutes or until piping hot.

Meanwhile, cut the bread into 1cm/1/2in slices and toast lightly. Place on a serving platter and drizzle with the remaining oil. Top with the mushroom mixture and serve immediately, garnished with the basil sprigs. *Serves 4.*

NOTE This dish can be prepared ahead of time and reheated in an oven at 190°C/375°F/gas mark 5 for 15 minutes.

# Herb & Goat's Cheese Salad

**Marinade**

5 tablespoons walnut oil

3 tablespoons orange juice

1 tablespoon grated orange zest

1 tablespoon each chopped fresh
  coriander, parsley and mint

**Salad**

225g/8oz piece of goat's cheese log

4 ripe pears, peeled, cored and sliced

2–3 tablespoons orange juice

115g/4oz rocket leaves

60g/2oz shelled pecan nuts, toasted

Grated zest of ½ orange

Place the marinade ingredients in a screw-top jar and shake vigorously. Cut the cheese into four equal pieces and put into a shallow dish. Pour over the marinade, cover and chill for at least 1 hour.

Preheat the oven to 190°C/375°F/gas mark 5. Drain the cheese, reserving the marinade. Arrange the cheese pieces in a lightly oiled baking pan (they should not be touching) and bake for 10 minutes.

Meanwhile, brush the pear slices with the orange juice and arrange on serving plates with the rocket leaves and pecans. Garnish with the orange zest. Top with the baked cheese. Serve immediately, with the reserved marinade as dressing. *Serves 4.*

# Tapenade

225g/8oz stoned black olives

45g/1½oz capers

1 tablespoon chopped fresh thyme

2 cloves garlic

1 teaspoon Dijon mustard

1 x 55g/2oz can anchovies in oil

About 150ml/¼ pint virgin olive oil
or Mediterranean-flavoured oil

2–3 tablespoons brandy

¼ teaspoon freshly ground
black pepper

½ tablespoon parsley, chopped

*I*n a food processor, blend the olives, capers, thyme, garlic, mustard and anchovies (with their oil) to a thick paste. Gradually blend in the olive oil in a thin steady stream to form a thick purée. Stir in the brandy and season with the pepper. Serve spread on toast, sprinkled with the parsley.

To keep, store in small jars covered with olive oil in the refrigerator for up to 2 weeks. *Serves 4.*

# Prawn Sesame Toasts

225g/8oz raw prawns, peeled
6 spring onions, trimmed
2 fresh green chillies, seeded
Pinch of salt
1 size 6 egg
1 tablespoon light soy sauce

1 tablespoon sesame oil
6 thin slices white bread
2 tablespoons sesame seeds
Sunflower oil for deep frying
1–2 chopped fresh red chillies

*I*n the bowl of a food processor, finely chop together the prawns, 3 spring onions, the chillies, and salt until well combined. Add the egg, soy sauce and sesame oil and blend for 30 seconds.

Cut the bread into thin strips, top with the prepared prawn mixture and sprinkle with sesame seeds. Chill for 30 minutes.

Heat sunflower oil in a wok or deep fryer until a square of bread will turn golden in 2–3 minutes, Fry the toasts in batches for 3–5 minutes or until golden. Drain and serve, garnished with the remaining spring onions cut into tassels and the chopped chillies. *Serves 4.*

# MAIN-COURSE SALADS

## Salad of Wilted Spinach & Sole

115g/4oz fresh chanterelle
  mushrooms
450g/1lb sole fillets, skinned
3 tablespoons seasoned flour
2 tablespoons stir-fry oil

340g/12oz baby spinach leaves
2 tablespoons orange juice
2 teaspoons grated orange zest
2 teaspoons sesame oil

Wipe and slice the mushrooms. Cut the sole crossways into 2cm/¾in wide strips and coat in seasoned flour. Add 1 tablespoon of stir-fry oil to a large frying pan and sauté the mushrooms over moderate heat for 2 minutes. Remove, then add ½ tablespoon of stir-fry oil and half the fish. Cook gently for 1 minute. Remove the fish from the pan and reserve. Add the remaining stir-fry oil to the pan. When hot, add the remaining fish and cook gently for 1 minute. Return the mushrooms and reserved fish to the pan with the orange juice, half the orange zest and the sesame oil, and heat through for 1 minute. Arrange the fish and the pan juices on a bed of spinach on a serving plate. Serve garnished with the remaining orange zest. *Serves 4.*

# *Citrus Salad with Fresh Pear Dressing*

Chicory leaves

1 head frisée or other curly-leaved
    lettuce

2 pink grapefruit, peeled
    and segmented

4 large oranges, peeled and segmented

1 Spanish or red onion, peeled
    and sliced

Few mint sprigs

**Dressing**

2 ripe pears

120ml/4floz walnut oil

4 tablespoons virgin olive oil

1 tablespoon sherry vinegar or
    oregano-flavoured vinegar

Pinch of salt and ¼ teaspoon freshly
    ground black pepper

Separate and rinse the chicory and frisée leaves, then arrange with the fruit and onion on a serving platter. Garnish with mint sprigs.

Peel and core the pears. In a food processor, gradually blend the pears with the walnut oil, then with the olive oil. Add the vinegar and seasoning and blend for 30 seconds or until smooth. Drizzle the dressing over the salad and decorate with more mint sprigs. *Serves 4.*

NOTE For a delicious change, try adding fresh cooked crab meat to the salad.

24

# Melon & Feta Cheese Medley

3 slices wholemeal bread, crusts
  trimmed

2 tablespoons walnut oil

60g/2oz walnut or pecan nut halves

1 Charentais melon

¼ watermelon

½ honeydew melon

½ head radicchio

½ head frisée

225g/8oz feta cheese, crumbled

85g/3oz Niçoise or Kalamata
  black olives

Few mint sprigs

### Dressing

3 tablespoons soured cream

4 tablespoons walnut oil

3 tablespoons blackberry vinegar
  or garlic vinegar

Pinch of salt and ¼ teaspoon freshly
  ground black pepper

D ice the bread. Heat the oil to moderately high in a small frying pan and fry the bread for 4 minutes, stirring frequently, until crisp and golden brown. Add the nuts and cook for 30 seconds. Drain well.

Seed the melons, peel and cut into small wedges. Rinse the salad leaves and arrange on a serving platter. Top with the melon, cheese and olives, then scatter over the croûtons and nuts.

Gradually blend the soured cream with the oil. Stir in the vinegar and seasoning. Drizzle the dressing over the salad. Tear the mint, sprinkle over and serve, with warm crusty bread. *Serves 4–6.*

# Salad of Duck Breast with Mango & Kumquats

*4 duck breasts*
*Sea salt and freshly ground black pepper*
*2 tablespoons garlic-flavoured olive oil*
*1 tablespoon acacia honey*
*6 tablespoons mango or orange juice*
*1 ripe (but firm) mango, peeled, stoned and sliced*
*5–6 kumquats, thickly sliced*
*Sorrel leaves*
*2 teaspoons balsamic vinegar*
*½ tablespoon finely chopped fresh tarragon leaves*

*W*ipe the duck breasts, make 3 deep slashes across each, season to taste and place in a dish. Blend the oil with the honey and juice, pour over the duck, cover and marinate for 1 hour, turning occasionally. Drain, reserving the marinade.

In a frying pan, dry-fry the duck over moderately high heat until browned all over. Pour off the fat that has accumulated. Add the marinade, reduce the heat to moderately low and cook for 10 minutes. Add the mango and kumquats and continue to cook for 3–4 minutes. Remove the duck breasts, slice thinly crossways, and arrange on a bed of sorrel leaves. With a slotted spoon, transfer the fruit to the platter.

26

Skim the fat from the pan juices, then boil the juices on high heat until reduced by half. Remove from the heat, stir in the balsamic vinegar and pour over the duck. Garnish with the chopped tarragon. *Serves 4.*

NOTE The duck can be replaced by 4 rabbit pieces. Brown the rabbit in a nonstick frying pan with 2 tablespoons olive oil, then continue cooking as for the duck.

# Warm Seafood & Wild Mushroom Salad

*450g/1lb mixed raw seafood such as oysters, squid,*
*king prawns or crayfish and scallops*
*120ml/4floz garlic-flavoured olive oil or Mediterranean-flavoured oil*
*2 shallots, peeled and finely chopped*
*2 cloves garlic, crushed*
*1–2 canned jalapeño peppers, seeded and chopped*
*1–2 fresh green chillies, seeded and chopped*
*115g/4oz fresh chanterelles, wiped and sliced*
*5 tablespoons dry white wine*
*Dash of Tabasco sauce*
*Salad leaves*
*Shavings of black truffle or diced black olives*
*½ tablespoon chopped flat-leaved parsley*
*Few chervil sprigs*

*I*f using oysters, remove from the shell just before cooking. For squid, pull the sac and tentacles apart. Remove the backbone and innards from the sac and discard the head. Rinse the sac and tentacles, then slice and cook in boiling salted water for 3 minutes over high heat; drain. For prawns or crayfish, discard the heads, the fine legs, upper shell and the dark

28

intestinal vein running down the back. For scallops, discard the membrane around the white meat.

Heat the oil in a frying pan and over moderate heat sauté the shallots, garlic, jalapeños and chillies for 2 minutes. Add the mushrooms and continue to cook for 3 minutes or until softened. Remove from the pan with a slotted spoon, then stir in all seafood, except the oysters. Sauté the seafood for 3–4 minutes or until the crustaceans have turned pink. Add the oysters and cook for 1 minute more. Return the mushroom mixture to the pan and add the white wine and Tabasco sauce.

Increase the heat to high and continue to cook for 1 minute. Spoon on to a warmed serving platter lined with the salad leaves. Sprinkle with the shavings of truffle, chopped parsley and chervil.

*Serves 4.*

# Garlic-roasted Peppers

1 each red, green, yellow and
  orange pepper, seeded and cut
  into strips
1 courgette, thickly sliced
1 large onion, sliced
2 cloves garlic, crushed
4 tablespoons olive oil

¼ teaspoon freshly ground
  black pepper
1 tablespoon sesame seeds
Focaccia or ciabatta bread
10 black olives, pitted
Few oregano sprigs

*P*reheat the oven to 200°C/400°F/gas mark 6. Place the peppers in a roasting tin with the courgette, onion and garlic. Drizzle with the oil and sprinkle with the black pepper. Roast the peppers uncovered for 40 minutes, or until the vegetables have softened but are still firm. Sprinkle with the sesame seeds 5 minutes before the end of cooking.

Drizzle the focaccia with the pan juices, top with the roasted peppers and garnish with the olives and oregano. *Serves 4.*

# Warm Tomato Salad

*8 artichoke hearts, preserved in oil, drained*
*1 small ripe pineapple, peeled, cored and thinly sliced into rounds*
*2 beefsteak tomatoes, thinly sliced*
*225g/8oz smoked mozzarella cheese, thinly sliced*
*1 Spanish or red onion, thinly sliced*
*Few basil sprigs*

### Vinaigrette
*½ teaspoon mustard powder*
*1 teaspoon acacia honey*
*5 tablespoons basil-flavoured olive oil*
*3 tablespoons balsamic vinegar*
*Pinch of salt and ¼ teaspoon freshly ground black pepper*

Cut the artichokes in half and arrange on a serving platter together with the pineapple, tomatoes, cheese and onion.

In a small saucepan, blend the mustard with the honey and oil, then stir in the vinegar and seasoning. Heat through gently and stir until thoroughly blended. Pour the dressing over the salad and garnish with the basil sprigs. Serve immediately. *Serves 4.*

# Tabbouleh

*225g/8oz burghul wheat*
*120ml/4floz boiling water*
*5 tablespoons extra-virgin olive oil*
*2–3 tablespoons pine nuts*
*6 spring onions, trimmed and sliced diagonally*
*½ small cucumber, diced*
*225g/8oz cherry tomatoes, halved*
*45g/1½oz raisins*
*45g/1½oz Niçoise or Kalamata black olives*
*5 tablespoons chopped fresh mint*
*4 tablespoons chopped fresh parsley*
*4 tablespoons lime juice*
*Pinch of salt and ½ teaspoon freshly ground black pepper*
*60g/2oz mixed salad leaves or baby spinach leaves*
*4 lime wedges*
*Few mint sprigs*

*R*inse the burghul, then place in a bowl and cover with the boiling water. Let sit for 20 minutes or until the water has been absorbed. Drain well, then toss with a fork until the grains are fluffy and separate. Heat 1 tablespoon of the oil in a frying pan over moderate heat, add the pine nuts and sauté for 5 minutes. When golden, drain them on paper towels. Cool, then

32

stir into the burghul wheat.

Add the spring onions, cucumber, and cherry tomatoes to the burghul. Add the raisins, olives and herbs.

Mix the remaining olive oil with the lime juice. Add the seasoning, then pour over the burghul mixture and toss lightly together. Line a serving bowl with the washed salad leaves or baby spinach. Spoon the tabbouleh into the bowl and garnish with the lime wedges and mint sprigs. *Serves 4.*

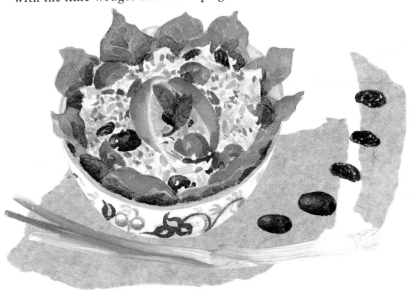

# Nutty Avocado Salad

4 large ripe avocados
Juice of 2 limes
5 tablespoons hazelnut oil
45g/1½oz mixed unsalted nuts such
    as almonds and cashews
60g/2oz sorrel or baby spinach
    leaves, rinsed

225g/8oz cottage cheese
115g/4oz seedless grapes
Pinch of salt and ¼ teaspoon freshly
    ground black pepper
1 teaspoon maple syrup

C ut the avocados in half, remove the stones, and peel and slice them. Sprinkle the slices with 1 tablespoon of lime juice; reserve the remaining juice.

Heat 1 tablespoon oil over moderate heat, add the nuts and gently sauté until lightly browned. Drain on paper towels.

Arrange the salad leaves on a serving platter and top with the avocados, nuts, cottage cheese and grapes. Place the remaining lime juice, oil, seasoning and maple syrup in a jar and shake, then drizzle over salad. *Serves 4.*

# Carpaccio Salad

*170g/6oz beef fillet*
*120ml/4fl oz extra-virgin olive oil or Italian-flavoured oil*
*Grated zest and juice of 1 large lemon*
*3 tablespoons chopped fresh parsley*
*3 tablespoons capers, coarsely chopped*
*85g/3oz mixed salad leaves*
*4 lemon wedges*

Slice the beef as thinly as possible, then place it between sheets of non-stick parchment and beat with a mallet until wafer-thin. Transfer the slices to a shallow dish.

Mix together the oil, zest and juice of lemon, parsley and capers. Pour the mixture over the beef, cover and marinate in the refrigerator for at least 6 hours. Remove the meat from the marinade with a slotted spoon. Toss the salad leaves with the marinade and arrange on a platter. Cover attractively with the carpaccio slices and garnish with lemon wedges. *Serves 4.*

# Sautéed Chicken Salad

*340g/12oz chicken breasts, skinned and boned*
*115g/4oz sun-dried tomatoes, coarsely chopped*
*5 tablespoons virgin olive oil or tomato-flavoured oil*
*3 tablespoons red wine vinegar*
*1 tablespoon acacia honey*
*115g/4oz shiitake mushrooms, wiped and thinly sliced*
*8 spring onions, trimmed and sliced diagonally*
*¼ teaspoon sea salt*
*3 tablespoons mixed peppercorns*
*60g/2oz mixed salad leaves*
*½ tablespoon chopped fresh basil and parsley*
*3 each red and yellow cherry tomatoes, quartered*

Cut the chicken meat into thin strips and put into a shallow dish with the sun-dried tomatoes. Mix 4 tablespoons oil with the vinegar and honey and pour over the chicken and tomatoes. Cover and marinate in the refrigerator for 3 hours, turning occasionally.

Drain the chicken and tomatoes, reserving the marinade. In the remaining oil, sauté the chicken for 5–8 minutes over moderately high heat,

stirring frequently. Add the mushrooms and continue to sauté for 3 minutes. Add the spring onions, season with the salt and stir in the peppercorns together with 4 tablespoons of reserved marinade. Stir for 2 minutes more. Line a serving platter with the salad leaves. Arrange the hot chicken mixture on top, then garnish with a sprinkling of the herbs and cherry tomatoes. *Serves 4.*

# MAIN DISHES

## Lobster & Cucumber Sauté

1 onion, sliced
3 celery stalks, trimmed
2 bay leaves
Few parsley sprigs
150ml/¼ pint dry white wine
1 tablespoon white wine vinegar
1.2 litres/2 pints water
2 large live lobsters
1 small cucumber, peeled
5 tablespoons basil-flavoured olive oil
1 Spanish or red onion, sliced

1 yellow pepper, seeded and
   cut into strips
Grated zest and juice of 1 lime
Pinch of salt and ¼ teaspoon freshly
   ground black pepper
Few basil sprigs
450g/1lb fresh pasta such as
   green and white fettucine,
   freshly cooked and drained

$P$lace the sliced onion, celery, herbs, white wine, vinegar and water in a large pan. Bring to the boil, turn down the heat to low and simmer gently for 15 minutes. Return to the boil and add the lobsters. Reduce heat to moderately low, cover and cook for 15 minutes or until the lobsters have turned bright orange-red. Remove

from the heat and allow to rest for 5 minutes. Remove from the pan and leave to cool. Remove the lobster meat, cut it into bite-size pieces and reserve.

Cut the cucumber into strips about 5cm/2in long. Heat the oil in a wok or large frying pan and sauté the onion over moderate heat for 3 minutes. Add the cucumber and pepper and continue to sauté for 5 minutes until the cucumber begins to become translucent. Stir in the lobster meat, grated lime zest and juice and seasoning. Sauté for 3 minutes or until piping hot. Tear the basil leaves, add to the wok or pan and stir once more. Serve immediately, with the pasta. *Serves 4.*

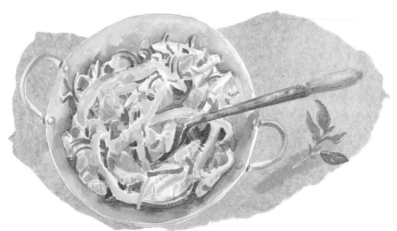

## *Beef Brochettes on Wilted Rocket*

340g/12oz beef fillet

4 tablespoons sesame oil

3 tablespoons soy sauce

2 cloves garlic, crushed

Grated zest and juice of 1 large orange

1 tablespoon orange blossom honey

2 bay leaves

1 large orange

3 tablespoons garlic-flavoured olive oil

3 tablespoons pine nuts

225g/8oz rocket or baby spinach

4 orange twists

*D*iscard any fat from the beef. Cut the meat into 5cm/2in cubes and place it in a shallow dish. Put the sesame oil, soy sauce, garlic, grated orange zest and juice and the honey in a small saucepan. Stir over moderately hight heat until thoroughly blended. Allow to cool before pouring over the beef cubes. Add the bay leaves, cover and marinate the meat in the refrigerator for at least 2 hours, or longer if time permits.

Preheat the grill to high. Cut the orange into wedges. Drain the beef and thread the meat and orange on to skewers. Reserve the marinade. Grill for 6–8 minutes, turning frequently and brushing with the reserved marinade, until cooked to your taste. Keep warm while cooking the rocket.

Heat the olive oil in a frying pan over moderate heat and stir-fry the pine nuts for 1–2 minutes until golden. Add the rocket and continue to stir-fry for 30 seconds or until just wilted. Arrange on a serving platter and top with the skewered brochettes. Garnish with the orange twists. *Serves 4.*

NOTE For an interesting variation, substitute 2 tablespoons toasted sesame seeds for the pine nuts.

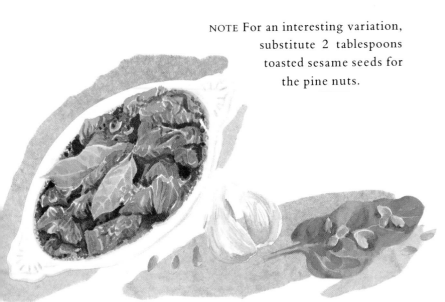

41

# Fettucine with Mushroom-Basil Sauce

### Sauce

*120ml/4floz basil-flavoured olive oil*
*2 cloves garlic, crushed*
*225g/8oz button mushrooms, wiped and thinly sliced*
*2–3 tablespoons pine nuts*
*Grated zest and juice of ½ lime*
*30g/1oz finely chopped fresh basil leaves*
*3 tablespoons finely chopped fresh mint leaves*
*115g/4oz pecorino cheese, grated*
*3 tablespoons crème fraîche*
*Pinch of salt and ¼ teaspoon freshly ground black pepper*

*340g/12oz fresh fettucine or other fresh pasta*
*Few basil sprigs*

*F*or the sauce, heat 3 tablespoons of the oil over moderate heat, add the garlic and mushrooms and cook for 2 minutes. Stir in the pine nuts, lime zest and juice and herbs. Add the remaining oil, half of the cheese, the crème fraîche and seasoning.

Meanwhile, cook the pasta in boiling salted water over high heat for 3–5 minutes until *al dente,* then drain. Toss with the sauce and serve garnished with basil sprigs and the remaining grated pecorino cheese. *Serves 4.*

# Gnocchi with Mushroom-Basil Sauce

225g/8oz ricotta cheese

60g/2oz butter

5 tablespoons grated Parmesan cheese

2 size 5 eggs, beaten

85–115g/3–4oz flour

¼ teaspoon each salt and freshly ground black pepper

300ml/½ pint Mushroom-Basil Sauce (see recipe opposite), to serve

*M*ix all the ingredients in a bowl and beat until smooth. Form into small balls with your hands, then roll them in a little flour. Poach the gnocchi a few at a time in gently boiling water for about 5 minutes, or until they rise to the top. Drain and toss gently with the prepared Mushroom-Basil Sauce. *Serves 4.*

# Roasted Tuna with Walnuts

4 tuna steaks, wiped dry

2 bay leaves, coarsely torn

Few mixed peppercorns, bruised

2 shallots, sliced

6 tablespoons walnut oil

3 tablespoons lemon juice

**Walnut Sauce**

3 tablespoons walnut oil

15g/½oz unsalted butter

1 small onion, finely chopped

2 cloves garlic, crushed

30g/1oz walnut halves, chopped

30g/1oz Parmesan cheese, grated

120ml/4floz crème fraîche

Pinch of salt and ¼ teaspoon freshly
    ground black pepper

½ tablespoon chopped fresh herbs,
    such as parsley, tarragon or mint

4 lemon twists

*P*lace the tuna in a shallow dish and scatter the bay leaves, peppercorns and shallots over them. Mix the walnut oil with the lemon juice. Pour over, cover and marinate in the refrigerator for at least 1 hour, turning once or twice.

When ready to cook, preheat the oven to 180°C/350°F/gas mark 4. Take a large sheet of foil and place in a roasting tin. Using a fish slice, place the tuna and shallots on the foil. Pour over a little of the marinade, then seal the foil to completely enclose the tuna. Roast for 20–25 minutes or until the fish is opaque and cooked through.

To make the sauce, heat the oil and butter in a small saucepan over medium heat. Gently sauté the onion and garlic for 5 minutes. Add the walnuts and continue cooking for 3 minutes more. Stir in the cheese, crème fraîche, and the seasoning. Heat through until well blended and piping hot. Brush the tuna with the sauce and garnish with the fresh minced herbs and the lemon twists. *Serves 4.*

# Poussins with Orange

*4 poussins*
*1 teaspoon salt and ½ teaspoon freshly ground black pepper*
*120ml/4floz olive oil*
*Grated zest and juice of 1 large orange*
*3 tablespoons orange blossom honey*
*4 tablespoons mixed fresh peppercorns*
*1 teaspoon finely chopped fresh coriander*
*115g/4oz salad leaves*
*4 orange slices*
*1 tablespoon fresh parsley, finely chopped*

*P*lace the poussins, breast down, on a board. With poultry shears, cut along each side of the backbones and discard. Open up the birds and snip out the wishbones. Turn them over, push down sharply to break the breastbones and flatten the birds. Rinse and dry.

Thread a skewer through one wing, both breasts and the other wing of each bird. Repeat with the legs. Season with the salt and pepper and place in a large shallow dish. Repeat with the remaining three birds.

Mix together the oil, orange zest and juice and honey in a saucepan. Heat through over moderately high heat

46

until well mixed, then stir in 1 tablespoon of the fresh peppercorns and the coriander. Allow to cool before pouring over the poussins. Cover and marinate in the refrigerator for at least 2 hours, turning at least once.

Preheat the grill to moderate. Drain the poussins, reserving the marinade, and scatter the remaining peppercorns over the birds. Place them skin side down in the grill pan. Grill for 10 minutes, then turn, brush with reserved marinade and grill for a further 8–10 minutes or until birds are cooked through. Remove the skewers and serve the poussins on a bed of the salad leaves, garnished with the orange slices and parsley. *Serves 4.*

# *Chicken with Rosemary*

*675g/1½lb waxy potatoes*
*3 small Spanish or red onions*
*4–5 cloves garlic*
*½ teaspoon freshly milled sea salt*
*Few rosemary sprigs*
*150ml/¼ pint olive oil or rapeseed oil*
*4 chicken breast halves, boned*
*½ teaspoon freshly ground black pepper*

Preheat the oven to 200°C/400°F/gas mark 6. Peel the potatoes and cut into 1cm/½in cubes. Rinse well in cold water, dry on a clean tea towel and put in a roasting tin. Peel 2 of the onions and cut into small wedges. Peel and finely chop 3 of the garlic cloves. Scatter the onion and garlic over the potatoes and season with half the salt. Tear half the rosemary sprigs into small pieces and sprinkle over the vegetables. Pour half of the oil over the potatoes. Roast in the oven for 45 minutes, turning the potatoes occasionally.

Meanwhile, rinse and wipe the chicken breasts. Peel the remaining garlic, cut into slivers and insert into cuts made in the chicken breasts. Season with the remaining salt and the pepper. Place the breasts on a metal rack and brush all over with 3 tablespoons of the remaining oil. Position the rack over the

48

potatoes and roast for 20 minutes or until thoroughly cooked but not dry. Brush the breasts with oil at least twice during roasting. Serve the chicken and potatoes garnished with the remaining rosemary sprigs, and onion cut into rings. *Serves 4.*

NOTE The chicken will be more succulent if roasted with the skin on, but it can be prepared with boneless, skinless chicken breasts. For an alternative, turkey breasts may be substituted for the chicken. They will need closer watching as turkey is a drier meat.

# Squid & Prawn Stir-fry

*225g/8oz prepared squid*
*225g/8oz raw king prawns*
*2–3 fresh green chillies, seeded and coarsely chopped*
*2 cloves garlic, crushed*
*1 tablespoon peeled and freshly grated root ginger*
*Grated zest and juice of 2 limes*
*½ teaspoon freshly ground black pepper*
*5 tablespoons chilli oil*
*3 tablespoons chopped fresh coriander*
*10 spring onions, trimmed*
*200g/7oz sugar snap peas*
*115g/4oz baby sweetcorn*
*1 tablespoon Thai fish sauce*
*2 teaspoons sesame oil*

*L*ightly rinse the squid and cut it into 2.5cm/1in slices. Remove the head and fine legs from the prawns. Using sharp scissors or a knife, cut the prawns lengthways down the back until almost in half, but leave the tail intact. Remove and discard the intestinal vein. Rinse the prawns lightly.

Arrange the squid and prawns in a shallow dish. Mix together the chillies, garlic, grated ginger, zest of 1 lime and black pepper. Sprinkle over the squid and prawns. Mix 4 tablespoons of the chilli oil with the lime juice and coriander. Pour over the seafood, cover and chill for at least 1 hour.

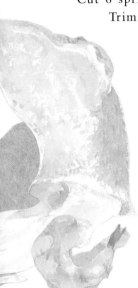

Cut 6 spring onions diagonally into 1cm/½in pieces. Trim the sugar snap peas and cut in half. Drain the seafood. Heat the remaining chilli oil in a wok over high heat until almost smoking, then stir-fry the squid and prawns for 2 minutes. Reduce the heat to moderately high, add the vegetables and stir-fry for 2 minutes. Pour in the fish sauce and continue to stir-fry for 1 minute. Add the sesame oil, give one last stir, then serve immediately, garnished with the remaining grated lime zest and 4 spring onions, cut into tassels. *Serves 4.*

# Turkey Julienne with Steamed Baby Vegetables

*450g/1lb mixed fresh baby vegetables, such as broad or French beans,*
*carrots, cauliflower, aubergines, courgettes, and patty pan squash*
*340g/12oz turkey breast, skinned and boned*
*4 tablespoons hazelnut oil*
*2 tablespoons coarsely chopped hazelnuts*
*2 teaspoons whole grain mustard*
*Grated zest of 1 lemon*
*1 tablespoon balsamic vinegar*
*4 tablespoons crème fraîche*
*Few chervil sprigs*

Prepare the vegetables. If using fresh broad beans, shell, then split the outer casing on each bean. Discard the casing and reserve the two halves inside. Trim the French beans; trim and clean the carrots; and score the skins of the courgettes in a decorative fashion. Cut the cauliflower into tiny florets; rinse the aubergines and patty pan squash and trim the tops.

Place the vegetables (in order of time required for steaming) in a steamer containing simmering water. Steam over low heat for up to 10 minutes or until vegetables are just tender-crisp.

Meanwhile, cut the turkey meat into thin strips about 7.5cm/ 3in. Heat 1 tablespoon of oil in a wok or frying pan and lightly

sauté the hazelnuts over moderately high heat for 1 minute or until toasted. Drain and reserve. Add the remaining oil to the pan and stir-fry the turkey over high heat for 4–5 minutes or until cooked through. Add the mustard and lemon zest, cook for 1 minute; remove from the heat. Stir in the vinegar and crème fraîche. Return to low heat and stir gently until warm. Place the steamed vegetables round the edge of a warm serving platter and spoon the turkey and sauce into the centre. Sprinkle with the toasted hazelnuts, garnish with chervil sprigs and serve. *Serves 4.*

## Pan-fried Salmon

4 salmon steaks, about 170g/6oz each
¼ teaspoon salt and ½ teaspoon
   freshly ground black pepper
Juice of 1 lime
4 tablespoons hazelnut oil
60g/2oz skinned hazelnuts,
   coarsely chopped

15g/½oz unsalted butter
1 tablespoon each chopped fresh
   mint and parsley
4 lime wedges
Few dill sprigs

Season the salmon with the salt and pepper and sprinkle with the lime juice. Set aside. Heat 1 tablespoon oil in a frying pan and stir the nuts over moderately high heat for 1 minute. Drain and reserve.

Heat the remaining oil with the butter in the pan over moderately high heat, add the salmon and cook for 2–3 minutes on each side. Add the mint, parsley and nuts and continue to cook for 1 minute, or until done. Remove the fish from the pan, pour on the nutty sauce and garnish with the lime wedges and dill sprigs. *Serves 4.*

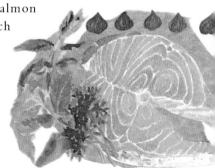

# DRESSINGS & PRESERVES

## Egg-safe Classic Mayonnaise

1 size 2 egg white

2 tablespoons lemon juice, or
  more if required

2 tablespoons water

2 teaspoons Dijon mustard

240ml/8floz olive oil

Pinch of salt

*M*ix the egg white with 2 tablespoons lemon juice. Cover tightly and refrigerate for at least 48 hours, or up to 4 days.

In a blender or food processor, whirl the acidified egg white with the water and mustard. With the motor running, add the oil in a slow steady stream, blending until emulsified. Season with salt and more lemon juice, if required; blend again. Keep, covered and chilled, up to 4 days. *Makes about 300ml/½ pint.*

NOTE If you wish to vary the flavour of the mayonnaise, substitute another oil for the olive oil, or vinegar for the lemon juice. Try combining hazelnut oil with balsamic vinegar, or Mediterranean-flavoured oil with a good red wine vinegar. Stir finely chopped fresh herbs — such as parsley, chervil or basil — or flavourings — such as watercress, horseradish, blue cheese or capers — into the basic mayonnaise.

## Egg-safe Saffron & Chilli Mayonnaise

Size 2 egg white
2 tablespoons lime juice
2 tablespoons water
Pinch of chilli powder
1 teaspoon saffron threads

½ teaspoon mustard powder
150ml/¼ pint extra-virgin olive oil
   or rapeseed oil
Few drops of chilli oil
Pinch of salt

*M*ix the egg white with the lime juice. Cover tightly and refrigerate for at least 48 hours, or up to 4 days.

In a blender or food processor, whirl the acidified egg white with the water, chilli powder, saffron and mustard powder. With the motor running, add the olive or rapeseed oil, then the chilli oil. Blend until emulsified. Season with salt and blend again. Keep, covered and chilled, up to 4 days. *Makes about 240ml/8floz.*

# Chile & Orange Vinaigrette

*1 teaspoon whole grain mustard*
*1–1½ teaspoons dark brown sugar*
*¼ teaspoon salt and ½ teaspoon freshly ground black pepper*
*1–2 serrano chiles, seeded and finely chopped*
*Grated zest and juice 1 large orange*
*3 tablespoons virgin olive oil*

*P*ut all the ingredients into a screwtop jar and shake vigorously. Let stand at least 1 hour to allow the flavours to blend. *Makes about 150ml/¼ pint.*

NOTE This dressing is very flavourful, but still versatile enough to partner all manner of salad bowl ingredients. Try it tossed with a simple salad of sliced tomatoes, avocados and lettuce leaves. It could also be used to dress a hearty salad of cold steamed baby potatoes, diced cooked chicken, cooked kidney beans and finely chopped red onion, garnished with a sprinkling of chopped fresh coriander.

# Strawberry Vinaigrette

*115g/4oz ripe strawberries*
*2 tablespoons fresh orange juice*
*1 teaspoon clear honey*
*1 teaspoon Dijon mustard*
*Pinch of salt and ¼ teaspoon freshly ground black pepper*
*3 tablespoons sunflower oil*
*1 tablespoon balsamic vinegar*

Purée the strawberries with the orange juice and honey. Press through a fine-mesh sieve to remove any seeds. Mix the mustard with the seasoning in a bowl. Blend in the oil, followed by the strawberry purée and vinegar. Stir well before using. *Makes about 150ml/¼ pint.*

NOTE This vinaigrette can also be made with other berries, such as raspberries, blackberries or blueberries. Be sure to taste as sweetness may need adjusting. It is delicious with cooked chicken or fish served on a bed of greens, or drizzled over spears of steamed asparagus.

# *Lime & Coriander Vinaigrette*

*Pinch of chilli powder*
*Pinch of salt*
*1 teaspoon peeled and finely grated root ginger*
*1 teaspoon clear honey*
*120ml/4floz garlic-flavoured olive oil*
*4 tablespoons lime juice*
*1 tablespoon chopped fresh coriander*

*M*ix the chilli powder, salt, ginger and honey together, then blend in the olive oil and lime juice. Add the coriander, stir and use as soon as possible. *Makes just over 180ml/6floz.*

# Preserved Mixed Vegetables in Oil & Rosemary

*450g/1lb aubergines, trimmed*
*450g/1lb courgettes, trimmed*
*2 tablespoons salt*
*450g/1lb mixed colour peppers, seeded*
*1.35 litres/2¼ pints white vinegar*
*600ml/1 pint water*
*4 bay leaves*
*4 cloves*
*8 peppercorns*
*600–750ml/1–1¼ pints olive oil*
*3–4 cloves garlic, crushed*
*About 12 rosemary sprigs*

Slice the aubergines and courgettes, sprinkle with salt and leave for 30 minutes. Drain and rinse thoroughly. Place the peppers under the grill preheated to high and cook for about 10 minutes, turning frequently, until the skins have blackened slightly. Cool, then peel and slice into strips.

Mix the vinegar with the water in a wide deep pan. Add the bay leaves and spices, bring to the boil over high heat and drop in the vegetables. Return to the boil, reduce the heat and simmer for 5 minutes; be sure that the vegetables are completely covered with the liquid at all times. Drain and leave until completely dry.

Pour a little of the oil into a sterilised jar. Arrange a layer of the vegetables on top. Sprinkle with a little of the garlic and a few rosemary sprigs. Cover with more oil. Continue layering until all the vegetables have been used. Top with oil, ensuring that the vegetables are completely immersed. Seal and label the jar. Store in a cool dark place for at least 1 month before using. Keep unopened for 3–6 months in a cool place. *Makes about 1.2 litres/2 pints.*

NOTE This is delicious as an antipasto, as part of a composed salad, or as a topping for crostini.

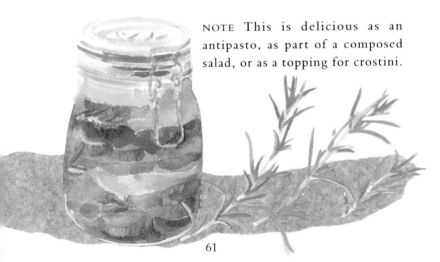

# Home-dried Tomatoes in Basil Oil

*900g/2lb tomatoes, ripe but firm and unblemished*
*1 teaspoon salt*
*1 teaspoon caster sugar*
*Few basil sprigs*
*450–600ml/¾–1 pint basil-flavoured olive oil*

Preheat the oven to 130°C/250°F/gas mark ½. Wash and dry the tomatoes, then cut them in half. Sprinkle the cut surfaces with the salt and sugar. Place cut side down on racks in baking trays. Place in the oven and dry out slowly for about 6–7 hours. Start checking after about 5 hours; the tomatoes should be dry and slightly chewy.

Pack into small sterilised jars, layering with sprigs of basil. Cover completely with the oil, seal and label. Keep for up to 6 months. *Makes about 4 small jars.*

# Preserved Mushrooms

*600ml/1 pint white wine vinegar*
*450ml/¾ pint water*
*1 tablespoon salt*
*12 bay leaves*
*6 each cloves and peppercorns*
*1 onion, sliced*
*8 fresh green chillies*
*900g/2lb assorted mushrooms,*
*wiped and sliced if large*
*450–600ml/¾–1pint olive oil*

Place the vinegar, water, salt, 5 bay leaves, the spices, onion and 4 chillies in a wide deep pan, bring to the boil and cook over high heat for 5 minutes. Reduce the heat and add the prepared mushrooms. Bring back to the boil, then reduce heat to low and simmer for 5 minutes. Drain the mushrooms, place between clean cloths or paper towels and leave for a few hours or until dry.

Spoon the mushrooms into sterilised jars, layered with the remaining bay leaves and chillies. Cover completely with the oil. Seal and label. Keep unopened for 3–6 months in a cool place. *Makes about 4 small jars.*

# Index